TJ Publishers

Advantage Business Centre

132-134 Great Ancoats Street

Manchester

M4 6DE

Tel: 0141 880 6839

Fax: 0870 124 9189

e-mail: teejaypublishers@btinternet.com

web page: www.teejaypublishers.co.uk

© TeeJay Publishers 2014
   First Edition published by TeeJay Publishers - January 2014

Printed by :-

Elanders Ltd
Merlin Way
New York Business Park
North Tyneside NE27 0QG
Registered in England number 3788582
 http://www.elanders.com/uk

Year 1
Textbook

Book 1B

Produced by members of the TeeJay Writing Group

T Strang, J Geddes and J Cairns.

TeeJay would like to thank *Caoimhe Ni Chomhrai* and *Rachel Phazey* for
their invaluable advice, recommendations and help with this book.

Front and Back Cover and web-site designed by *Fraser McKie*.
(http://www.frasermckie.com)

Characters in the book developed and drawn by
Susan Fitzpatrick and *Karen Anna Sandholm*.

National Curriculum TextBook 1B

- This book, along with Textbook 1A covers every outcome of the Year 1 course, as laid out in the National Curriculum England framework document, (September 2013).

- There are no A and B exercises. The book covers the 2nd half of the Year 1 course without the teacher having to pick and choose which questions to leave out and which exercises are important. They all are !

- The book follows on directly from TeeJay's Year 1 Book 1A and includes revision and consolidation of the work covered in Book 1A.

- Year 1 Book 1B contains a 10 page "Chapter 14" which primarily revises every topic from our Year 1 course and can be used as a diagnostic tool. This could be followed by TeeJay's diagnostic assessments* of the work covered in our Year 1 books.

- Non-calculator skills are emphasised and encouraged throughout the book.

- Each chapter will have a "Revisit - Review - Revise" exercise as a summary.

- Homework*, mirroring exercise by exercise, the topics in this book, is available as a photocopiable pack.

- TeeJay's Assessment Pack* for Year 1 work, is also available as a photocopiable pack, and can be used topic by topic or combined to form a series of Year 1 Cumulative Tests. It also contains a series of longer assessments covering the Outcomes as laid out in the National Curriculum England framework document.

We make no apologies for the multiplicity of colours used throughout the book, both for text and in diagrams - we feel it helps brighten up the pages !!

T Strang, J Geddes, J Cairns

(January 2014)

* Available for purchase separately.

Contents

The Family

Mr Duff   Mrs Todd   Mr Todd   Miss Smart

Denzel   Willis   Ravi   Nick   Tiddles   Ben   Spot   Lucy   Jane   Jemma   Sarah   Ella

Chapter 1

Addition Revision

Exercise 1

1. How many in total ?

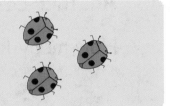

Set down like :-

$$\begin{array}{r} 5 \\ + 3 \\ \hline \end{array}$$

2. Find :-

a $\begin{array}{r} 11 \\ + 2 \\ \hline \end{array}$	b $\begin{array}{r} 12 \\ + 3 \\ \hline \end{array}$	c $\begin{array}{r} 14 \\ + 2 \\ \hline \end{array}$
d $\begin{array}{r} 10 \\ + 7 \\ \hline \end{array}$	e $\begin{array}{r} 5 \\ + 13 \\ \hline \end{array}$	f $\begin{array}{r} 7 \\ + 12 \\ \hline \end{array}$
g $6 + 4$	h $11 + 8$	i $8 + 12.$

3. Find the missing number :-

a $1 + \boxed{} = 9$

b $\boxed{} + 6 = 11$

c $3 + \boxed{} = 12$

d $\boxed{} + 10 = 18$

e $9 + \boxed{} + 4 = 15$

f $\boxed{} + 14 + 2 = 20.$

4. There are 16 apple trees and
   3 pear trees in a garden.

   How many trees is that in total ?

5.  A cat has 7 kittens.

   Another cat has 11 kittens.

   How many kittens altogether ?

6. There are 4 sweets in a jar.

   There are 15 sweets in a packet.

   How many sweets are there altogether ?

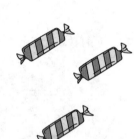

7. Jemma has 10 bows.

   Jane has the same number of bows.

   How many bows do they have altogether ?

8. 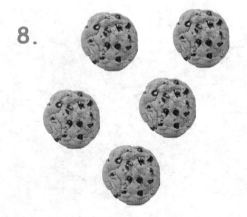 Mr Todd has 5 biscuits.

   Mrs Todd has 3 biscuits.

   Their children have 11 biscuits.

   How many biscuits does the
   family have ?

1. Find :-

| a 8 – 3 | b 5 – 2 | c 9 – 6. |

2. Copy and complete :-

a   13
    – 2
	b 18
	    – 4
		c 17
		    – 6

d   19
    – 9
	e 11
	    – 7
		f 14
		    – 8

g   14
    – 9
	h 18
	    – 9
		i 15
		    – 8

3. Find :-

a 15 – 3	b 18 – 7	c 15 – 5
d 13 – 6	e 19 – 7	f 16 – 4
g 14 – 7	h 17 – 1 – 4	i 15 – 8 – 7.

4. Jim has **17** tyres. Jeff takes **6** of them.

How many tyres does Jim have now ?

5. Sam has **20** tickets for a show.

   He gives **8** tickets to his family.

   How many tickets does he have left ?

6.  Mary has **16** strawberries.

   She eats **seven** of them.

   How many does she have left ?

7. a   Javin eats **8** of his **15** fish fingers.

   How many does he have left ?

   b      Sally has **17** dresses, Sue has **nine**.

   How many **more** does Sally have ?

8.   What is the missing number ?

   a   16 – ☐ = 12   b   ☐ – 2 = 7   c   ☐ – 4 = 9

   d   11 – ☐ = 2   e   ☐ – 8 = 8   f   16 – ☐ – 3 = 6.

9. Jason caught some fish.
   He gave Dez **9** of them.
   Jason now had **9** fish left.

   How many fish did Jason catch ?

A Mixture of Addition & Subtraction

1. Find :-

   a $8 + 2$ b $9 - 7$ c $5 + 4$ d $10 - 8.$

2. Copy and complete :-

   a $\begin{array}{r} 16 \\ -\ 4 \\ \hline \end{array}$ b $\begin{array}{r} 12 \\ +\ 4 \\ \hline \end{array}$ c $\begin{array}{r} 19 \\ -\ 6 \\ \hline \end{array}$

   d $\begin{array}{r} 14 \\ +\ 6 \\ \hline \end{array}$ e $\begin{array}{r} 13 \\ -\ 5 \\ \hline \end{array}$ f $\begin{array}{r} 14 \\ +\ 5 \\ \hline \end{array}$

   g $\begin{array}{r} 15 \\ -\ 7 \\ \hline \end{array}$ h $\begin{array}{r} 12 \\ +\ 8 \\ \hline \end{array}$ i $\begin{array}{r} 13 \\ -\ 4 \\ \hline \end{array}$

3. Find :-

   a $15 + 3$ b $19 - 5$ c $11 + 5$

   d $11 - 6$ e $11 + 7$ f $16 - 7$

   g $7 + 6 - 8$ h $11 + 8 - 7 + 1 - 6.$

4. Ted has 12 shirts. Six are worn and put in the bin.

   How many shirts does Ted have now ?

5. Mr Todd has **16** bottles of juice.

   At a party, he drinks **nine** of them.

   How many bottles does he have left ?

6.  Martin has **15** computer games.

   If he gives **eight** of them away,
   how many will he have left ?

7. Jai eats **7** of his **12** grapes.

   How many does he have left ?

8.  Len has **17** files, Louis has **nine**.

   How many **more** does Len have ?

9. What is the missing number ?

   a 11 – ☐ = 2   b ☐ + 8 = 15   c ☐ – 5 = 5

   d 11 + ☐ = 19   e ☐ – 8 = 12   f 11 – ☐ + 3 = 6.

10. Harry has **nineteen** mice.
    He gives some of them to Bert.
    Harry now has **eight** left.

    How many mice did he give to Bert ?

1. Copy and complete :-

a   15
     − 3

b   11
     + 5

c   20
     − 5

d   17
     − 7

e   12
     + 7

f   13
     − 8

g   18
     + 2

h   14
     − 9

i   15 − 6   j   13 + 7   k   12 + 6 − 8 + 2 − 5.

2. Find the missing number :-

a   2 + ☐ = 10   b   ☐ + 11 = 16   c   ☐ + 13 = 20

d   9 − ☐ = 3   e   ☐ − 4 = 11   f   ☐ + 14 − 2 = 15.

3. a   Alex has **12** coins. She loses **5** of them.

       How many coins does Alex have now ?

b      Bob had some apples.

       Kyle gave him **4** more apples.

       Bob then had a total of **twenty** apples.

       How many apples did Bob start with ?

Grouping in 2's

Be able to collect items in groups of 2.

You may use counters or coins to help.

Look at what happens when you have **pairs** of sets of coins :-

 + =   2 lots of **1** coin = 2 coins.   **2**

 + =    2 lots of **2** coins = 4 coins.   **4**

 + =   2 lots of **3** coins = 6 coins.   **6**

 +  =   2 lots of **4** coins = 8 coins.   **8**

What do you think **2** lots of **5** coins will be ?

Can you see how this pattern might continue ?

You may use counters or coins to help.

1. Sarah and Jane have the
   same number of dice each.

   a   How many does each have ?

   b   How many do they have
        altogether ?

   c   Copy and complete :- " 2 lots of 3 are ....".

2. a   How many wheels on this car ?

   b   How many will there be on
        2 cars ?

   c   Copy and complete :-

        " 2 lots of 4 are ....".

3. Ben and Nick both have the same size chocolate bar.

   a   How many squares are
        there on each bar ?

   b   How many squares have
        they altogether ?

   c   Copy and complete :-   " 2 lots of 6 are ....".

4. A lolly costs :-

   a   How much does the lolly cost ?

   b   What will the cost be for 2 lollies ?

   c   Copy and complete :- " 2 lots of 7 are ....".

5. Denzel and Willis each have a packet of Rolchies.

   Denzel opened his packet.

   a   How many Rolchies are in his packet ?

   b   How many Rolchies do they have altogether ?

   c   Copy and complete :- " 2 lots of 8 are ....".

6. Mr Todd uses this number of screws to put up a shelf.

   a   How many screws does he use for 1 shelf ?

   b   How many will he use for 2 shelves ?

   c   Copy and complete :- " 2 lots of 10 are ....".

7. a I have 2 lots of **1** coin.   How many coins in total ?

   b I have 2 lots of **2** coins. How many coins in total ?

8. How many coins in total ?

   a 2 lots of **3** coins.   b 2 lots of **4** coins.

   c 2 lots of **5** coins.   d 2 lots of **6** coins.

   e 2 lots of **7** coins.   f 2 lots of **8** coins.

   g 2 lots of **9** coins.   h 2 lots of **10** coins.

   i 2 lots of **11** coins.   j 2 lots of **12** coins.

9. a Write your answers to questions 7 and 8 like this :-

   | 2,   4,   6,   8, ... |

   b What do you notice about these numbers ?

10. a There are 2 CD's in a box.

    There are 4 boxes.

    How many CD's altogether ? (*Hint - 2 lots of 4*).

   b There are 2 light bulbs in a box.

    There are 7 boxes.

    How many light bulbs altogether ?

11. a  There are **2** shoes in a shoe box.

How many shoes in **8** boxes ?

b There are **2** dolls in a box.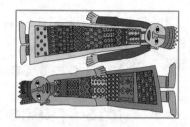

How many dolls in **ten** boxes ?

c 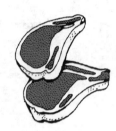 A packet holds **2** muffins.

How many muffins in **nine** packets ?

d There are **2** steaks in a packet.

How many steaks in **five** packets ?

12. Golf balls are sold in boxes of **two**.

How many golf balls are in **six** boxes ?

13. A large box can hold **2** teddy bears.

a How many teddies can **11** boxes hold ?

b How many boxes do I
need for **18** teddies ?

Double a Number

Using counters can help you when adding.

When you **double** a number you **add** it to itself.

Examples :- Double 3 = (3 + 3) = 6

Double 4 = (4 + 4) = 8

Double 5 = (5 + 5) = 10 .

Exercise 2

1. Find :-

a	double 2	b	double 3	c	double 4
d	double 5	e	double 6	f	double 7
g	double 8	h	double 9	i	double 10.

2. Here is a special dartboard.

    If a dart lands on **red** you **double** the score.

    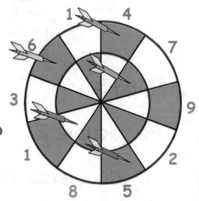

    a   What did the **purple** dart score ?

    b   What did the **blue** dart score ?

    c   What did the **brown** dart score ?

    d   What did the **green** dart score ?

    e   What did the **final** dart score ?

1. How many coins in total ?

   a   **2** lots of **3** coins.   b   **2** lots of **5** coins.

   c   **2** lots of **9** coins.   d   **2** lots of **2** coins.

2. a

   There are **2** bats in a box.

   How many bats in 6 boxes ?

  b   A bag of carrots weighs 2 kilograms.

     How many kilograms in **ten** bags ?

  c   A roller coaster chair holds **2** people.

     How many people in **eight** chairs ?

3. Find :-

   a double **2**   b double **1**   c double **5**

   d double **seven**   e double **nine**   f double **ten**.

4. When I double a number the answer is **22**.

   What number did I double ?

Length and Height 1

Know what is tall, small, long, short high, low, near, far, wide, narrow.

Comparing Lengths & Heights

Tall and Small

Jaki   Dave

Jaki is **tall**. Dave is **small**.

Jaki is taller than Dave.

Dave is **smaller** than Jaki.

High and Low

The doll is high.

The train is **low**.

The doll is higher than the train.

The train is **lower** than the doll.

Long and Short

The pencil is long. The eraser is **short**.

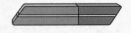

The pencil is longer than the eraser.

The eraser is **shorter** than the pencil.

Near and Far

Dodger is **near** the bowl.

Dodger

Rover is **far** away.

Dodger is **nearer** the bowl than Rover.

Rover

Rover is **further** from the bowl than Dodger.

Wide and Narrow

The door is **wide**. The window is **narrow**.

The door is **wider** than the window.

The window is **narrower** than the door.

Twice as and Half as ....

The door is **twice** as high as the girl.

The door is **twice** as wide as the window.

The girl is **half as** high as the door.

*You will meet **half** later in the book.*

1. Which is **taller** - A or B ?

a

b

2. Which is **smaller** - C or D ?

a

b

3. Which is **longer** - E or F ?

a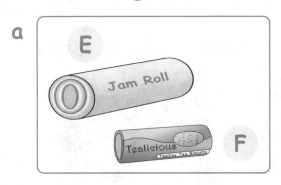

b

4. Which is **shorter** - G or H ?

a

b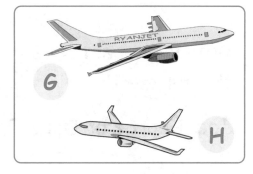

5. Which is **wider** - I or J ?

a  b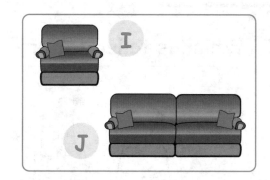

c   **Complete :-** The couch is t............ as long as the chair.

d   **Complete :-** The chair is h........ as long as the couch.

6. Which is **narrower** - K or L ?

a b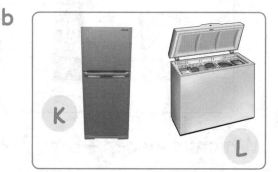

7. Who is **further** from the **red** house - Faye or Rita ?

8. Who is **nearest** the turkey -

Joe, George or Daisy ?

Length (a long time ago)

Be able to estimate and measure length using old units.

Many years ago, lengths (or distances) were measured in many different ways.

Here are three :-

Hand

hand-span

Pace

one step

Footstep

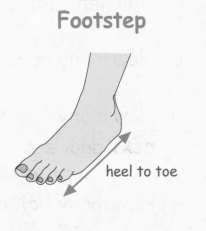

heel to toe

Exercise 2

1. a How many **hands** high do you think your desk is ?

   b How many **hands** high do you think your teacher is ?

   c How many **paces** do you think it is from the door to the back wall ?

   d How many **paces** do you think the length of the corridor is ?

   e How many **footsteps** do you think you would take to get to the door ?

2. Write down what you **think** the answer will be :-

a How many **footsteps** from your chair to the front of the room ?

b How many **hands** high is your teacher's table ?

c How many **paces** to walk around the room ?

d How many **footsteps** from your classroom to next door's ?

e How many **hands** across your desk ?

f How many **hands** high is your classroom door ?

g How many **paces** to walk round the school building ?

3. a **Measure** the lengths in **question 1** using the units.

b Find a few more old units used to measure lengths.

4. The above methods are **NOT** good ways of measuring length.

Discuss why not.

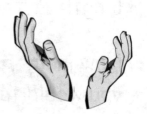

1. Which tyre is wider ?

2.  Which brush is shorter ?

3. Which insect is larger ?

4.  Which flower is smaller ?

5. a What is flying lowest ?

   b What is flying highest ?

   c Describe where the hot air balloon is.

 **Chapter 4**

Going Up in 2's, 5's and 10's

Recognise patterns of numbers going up in 2's, 5's and 10's.

Going Up in 2's

This number line shows the numbers from 0 up to 20.

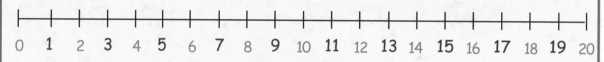

The number line goes on and on and on and on and.........

Look at this pattern -   0,   2,   4,   6,   8,   10, ...

The numbers in this pattern jump up in **2's**.

Another pattern -   1,   3,   5,   7,   9, ...

Again, the numbers in this pattern jump up in **2's**.

Example :-

Write the next three numbers in this pattern :-

24,   26,   28,   30, ..., ..., ...

The three numbers are :-   32,   34,   36.

The numbers in this pattern also jump up in 2's.

1. a   Write this pattern of numbers, going up in **2's** :-

   0,   2,   4,   6,   8,   10,   12, ..., ...,

   b   Continue the pattern up to 30.

2. a   Here is another pattern of numbers going up in **2's** :-

   1,   3,   5,   7,   9,   11, ..., ...,   Copy it.

   b   Continue the pattern up to 49.

3. Write down the next **3** numbers in each pattern of 2's :-

   a   18, 20, 22, ..., ..., ...   b   30, 28, 26, ..., ..., ...

   c   51, 53, 55, ..., ..., ...   d   89, 87, 85, ..., ..., ...

   e   76, 78, ..., ..., ...   f   73, 71, ..., ..., ...

4. What numbers are missing ?

   a   12 ☐ 16 18 ☐   b   17 ☐ 21 23 ☐

   c   ☐ 37 39 41 ☐   d   ☐ 78 76 74 ☐

   e   93 ☐ 89 87 ☐   f   ☐ 68 70 ☐ ☐ .

Worksheet 4·1

5. The numbers on the football tops go up in 2's.

   What are the missing numbers ?

6. The canoes have numbers 82, 80, 78, ... down to 68.

   What three numbers are missing ?

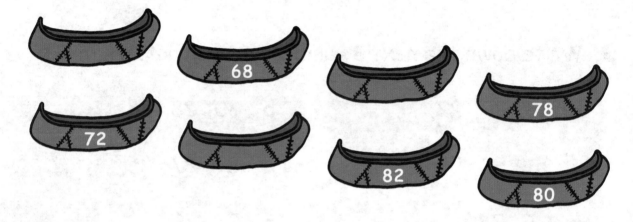

7. What number is **2 up** from 58 ?

   | 58 | ..... |

8. What number is **2 down** from 90 ?

   | ..... | 90 |

9. What number is **2 before**

   and what number is **2 after** 31 ?

   | ..... | 31 | ..... |

Going Up in 5's

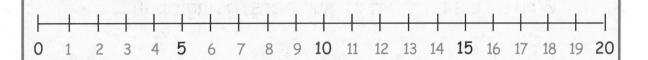

| 0 | 1 | 2 | 3 | 4 | 5 | 6 | 7 | 8 | 9 | 10 | 11 | 12 | 13 | 14 | 15 | 16 | 17 | 18 | 19 | 20 |

Look at the pattern -   0,   5,   10,   15, ...

The numbers in the pattern jump up in **5's**.

Example 1 :-

Write the next three numbers in the pattern :-

5,   10,   15,   20, ..., ..., ...

The three numbers are :-   25,   30,   35.

Going Up in 10's

Another pattern :-   0,   10,   20,   30, ...

Look !   The numbers in this pattern jump up in **10's** !

Example 2 :-

Write the next two numbers in the pattern :-

0,   10,   20,   30, ..., ...

The two numbers are :-   40   and   50.

1. a Write this pattern of numbers, going up in 5's :-

    0, 5, 10, 15, 20, ..., ..., ...

   b Continue the pattern up to 50.

2. a Write this pattern of numbers, also going up in 5's :-

    60, 65, 70, 75, ..., ..., ...

   b Continue the pattern up to 100.

3. Write down the next 3 numbers in each pattern of 5's :-

   a 10, 15, 20, ..., ..., ...   b 35, 40, 45, ..., ..., ...

   c 30, 25, 20, ..., ..., ...   d 75, 70, 65, ..., ..., ...

   e 20, 15, ..., ..., ...   f 95, 90, ..., ..., ...

4. What numbers are missing ?

   a 5 ☐ 15 ☐ 25   b 30 35 ☐ 45 ☐

   c ☐ 20 15 ☐ 5   d 50 45 ☐ ☐ 30

   e 65 ☐ 75 80 ☐   f ☐ 90 85 80 ☐ .

5. a Write this pattern of numbers, going up in 10's :-

0,   10,   20,   30, ..., ..., ...

b Continue the pattern up to 100.

6. What are the next 2 numbers in each pattern of 10's :-

a 30, 40, 50, ..., ...   b 60, 70, 80, ..., ...

c 40, 30, 20, ..., ...   d 100, 90, 80, ..., ...

7. Each pattern below goes up or down in 10's.

Write down the missing numbers :-

a 0 ☐ 20 30 ☐   b ☐ 60 70 ☐ 90

c 50 40 ☐ ☐ 10   d ☐ 80 70 ☐ 50.

8. Try this one :-

Both patterns below go up or go down in 10's.

Copy each pattern and put in the last two numbers :-

a 13,   23,   33,   43,   53,   63, ..., ...

b 97,   87,   77,   67,   57, ..., ...

9. Draw and colour the next 2 shapes in these patterns :-

a

b

c

d

10. Draw and colour the next 3 patterns for each shape :-

a

b

c

d

Odd and Even Numbers

Be able to recognise odd and even numbers.

Remember going up in 2's ?

There were 2 main patterns :-

> 0, 2, 4, 6, 8, 10, ...
>
> These are called EVEN numbers.
>
> All numbers ending in a 0, 2, 4, 6 or 8 are **even**.

and

> 1, 3, 5, 7, 9, 11, ...
>
> These are called **ODD numbers**.
>
> All numbers ending in a 1, 3, 5, 7 or 9 are **odd**.

Examples :-

> 76   (ends in a 6) - is an **even** number.
>
> 83   (ends in a 3) - is an **odd** number.
>
> 374 (ends in a 4) - is **even** !!!!

1. Write down :-

   a   all the **odd** numbers from 5 to 25.   (5, 7, ...)

   b   all the **even** numbers from 8 to 30.   (8, 10, ...)

2. a   Is **38** even or odd ?   b   Is **69** even or odd ?

3. What is the **4th** odd number ?

4. Choose **even** or **odd** :-

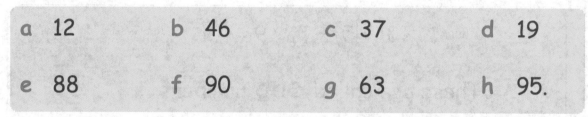

   a   12   b   46   c   37   d   19

   e   88   f   90   g   63   h   95.

5. Make a drawing of :-

   a   all the **even balls**

   b   all the **odd balls**.

6. Think of any **two odd numbers** .... and **add** them.

   Try this a few times with different **odd** numbers.

   Is your answer **always** even - or is it **always** odd ?

1. Write down the next 3 numbers in each pattern :-

   a   24, 26, 28, ..., ..., ...   b   30, 35, 40, ..., ..., ...

   c   60, 70, 80, ..., ..., ...   d   85, 80, 75, ..., ..., ...

2. What numbers are missing ?

   a   10 ☐ 20 ☐   b   ☐ 40 ☐ 60 70

   c   76 78 ☐ 82 ☐   d   ☐ 70 65 60 ☐

   e   100 ☐ 96 ☐   f   55 ☐ 35 25 ☐ .

3. What number is :-

   a   2 up from 48   b   **2 down** from 65

   c   5 up from 75   d   **5 down** from 90

   e   10 up from 70   f   **10 down** from 95 ?

4. a   Is 26 even or odd ?   b   Is 37 even or odd ?

5. What numbers are :-

   a   even

   b   odd ?

   12   34   76   50
   73   13
   81   97   45   68   25

Metric Length - Centimetres

Today, most lengths are measured using *metric* length.

A **ruler** measures small lengths in **centimetres**.

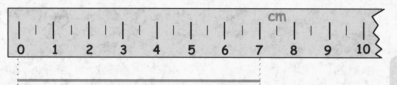

This red line is **7 cm** long.

Centimetres can be written as **cm**.

Exercise 1   *You will need a ruler.*

1. Write the lengths of these lines in centimetres (cm) :-

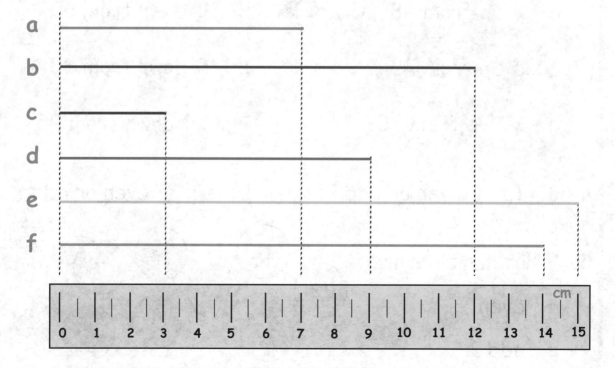

2. Use your ruler to measure each of these lines and write down your answer, to the nearest cm :-

a   _____

b   _____

c   _____

d   _____

e   _____

f   _____

3. Measure and write down the size of :-

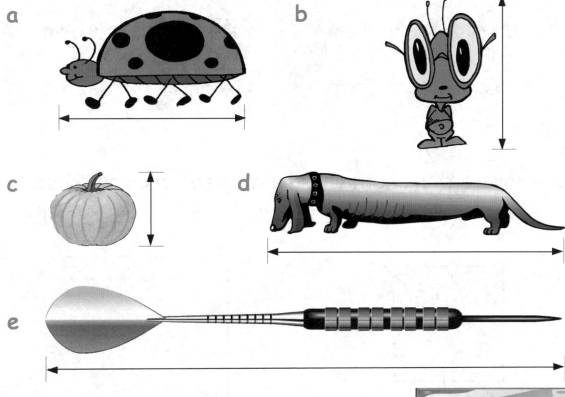

a

b

c

d

e

Worksheet 5·1

4. Make a **guess** at the length of each of these (in cm) :-

    a The **width** of this book. (*Across the page*).

    b The **length** of this book. (*Up and down the page*).

    c The **length** of your longest finger.

    d The **height** of your desk.

5. Use a ruler to **measure** each of the above (in question **4**) and write down your answers.

6. Use your ruler to **draw** and label lines which measure :-

a 3 cm	b 9 cm	c 14 cm	d 1 cm
e 16 cm	f 7 cm	g 4 cm	h 23 cm.

7. Measure the **length** and the **width** of each of these and write down your answers.

    a

square

    b

rectangle

7. c

rectangle

8. Now, take your time to draw all of the shapes in question 7 very, very carefully !

9. Use your ruler to draw each of the following :-

the diagrams are just sketches - NOT accurate !

a   A rectangle measuring 6 cm long and 2 cm wide.

2 cm

6 cm

b   A rectangle measuring 8 cm long and 5 cm wide.

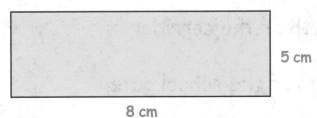

5 cm

8 cm

5 cm

c   A square with all its sides 5 cm.

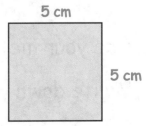

5 cm

Measuring in Metres

Be able to estimate and measure length using metres.

Sometimes for longer lengths, it is better to measure in **metres** (m).

A metre is **about** the distance from the ground to the handle on a door.

A **metre** is exactly 100 **centimetres**.

1 m = 100 cm

1 cm

| 10 | 20 | 30 | 40 | 50 | 60 | 70 | 80 | 90 | 100 |

1 metre

Exercise 2   *Ask your teacher for a 1 metre strip.*

1. Without measuring, **guess** (*to the nearest metre*) :–

   a the **height** of your desk   b the **height** of the ceiling

   c the **length** of your classroom

   d the **length** of the corridor

   e the **width** of the school gate.

2. Use your metre strip to measure **some** of the above.

   Write down your answers.

1. **Measure** and write down the length of the log.

2. a **Measure** the coloured lines below and write down each length, to the nearest cm.

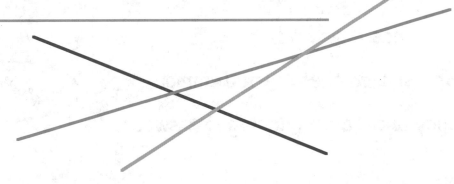

   b Which is the **longest** line ?

   c Which is the **shortest** line ?

3. How many **centimetres** make up a **metre** ?

4. a Draw a **rectangle** with length 6 cm and width 3 cm.

   b Draw a **square** with all sides of length 4 cm.

5. Would you measure the length of a swimming pool in **metres** or in **centimetres** ?

Chapter 6

Sharing Equally

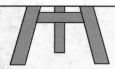

Be able to share an amount equally.

Sharing equally between 2 people means putting things into 2 piles so that each person would get the same amount.

Example 1 :-

Lucy has **2** sweets.

She shares them with Jemma.

Lucy and Jemma each get **1** sweet.

Example 2 :-

Nick has **4** marbles.

He shares them with Ben.

Nick and Ben each get **2** marbles.

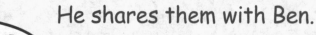

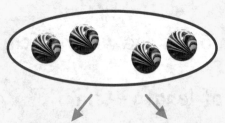

Exercise 1

You will need small cubes here, or coins or counters. Possibly work in pairs.

1. Jane has **6** dice.
   She shares them with Denzel.

   How many dice do Jane
   and Denzel get each.

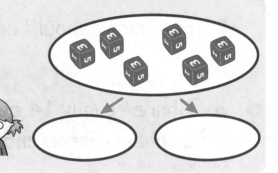

2. a **Count** out **8** small cubes,
   or coins, counters etc.

   b Share them **equally** between
   you and your friend.

   c How many of each did you get ?

3. a This time **count** out **10** small cubes.

   b Share them **equally** between
   you and your friend.

   c How many of each did you get ?

4. a   **Count** out **12** small counters
        and share them **equally**
        between two people.

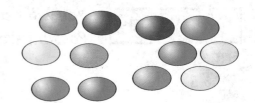

    b   How many should each person get ?

5. a   Share equally **14** buttons
        between Sarah and Ella.

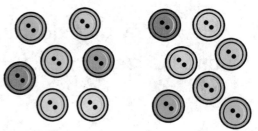

    b   How many should each person get ?

6. a   Share equally **16** pennies
        between Ben and Lucy.

    b   How many should each person get ?

7. a   **Six** cakes were shared
        between Avril and May.

        How many cakes did each get ?

    b   **8** sweets were shared
                                            equally between two girls.

                                            How many sweets did
                                            each girl get ?

8. Find answers to the following :-

   a 10 sweets were shared equally between 2 boys.

   How many sweets did each boy get ?

   b  18 T-shirts were placed equally into **two** drawers.

   How many were in each drawer ?

   c **Twelve** pencils were shared equally between **two** boys.

   How many did each boy get ?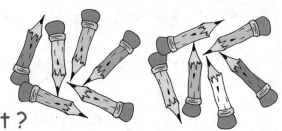

9. **Seven** cards are dealt equally between **two** boys.

   a How many will each get ?

   b How many will be left ?

10. **Nine** chocolates are shared equally between **two** girls.

   a How many will each girl get ?

   b How many will be left ?

Remember -

>   To *double* a number you add it to itself.

>   **Example :-**   Double 7 = (7 + 7) = **14**

11. Find :-

   a   double five   b   double 3

   c   double 4   d   double ten.

Extension work :-

To find **half** of a number of objects :-

   => you **share** it between **two** or **split** it in **two** .

Example :-   Find **half** of 8.

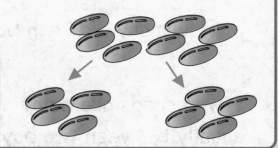

   From the picture :-

   half of 8 is 4.

12. Find :-

   a   half of 4   b   half of six   c   half of 12

   d   half of 2   e   half of ten   f   half of 0.

13. Ben got 20p for being good. Nick only got **half** of this.

   How much did Nick get ?

14. Lucy has 16 sweets. She gives **half** of them to Sarah.

   How many sweets does Lucy give to Sarah ?

1. Share 10 caramels between Jean and Jan.

   How many will they get each ?

2. What is :-

   a double 7   b double 9

   c half of 12   d half of 20 ?

3. Nine pears are split
   equally between two boys.

   a How many will each get ?

   b How many will be left ?

4. Eight plums are each split in half.

   How many pieces will there be ?

5. Simon has 20 pence.

   He gives half of this to Tracy.

   Tracy then gives half of what she has to Ken.

   How much does Ken get ?

Chapter 7

3 Dimensions

3D Shapes

Here are some **2 dimensional (2D)** shapes.

Can you remember the names of these flat shapes ?

 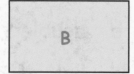 

Choose from Rectangle, Circle, Triangle and Square.

Discuss which one is which :- A is a ...., B is ....

Now we look at **solid 3 Dimensional (3D)** shapes.

You have seen them before, but may not know their names.

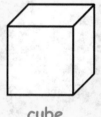 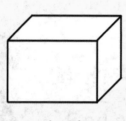  

| cube | cuboid | cone | cylinder |

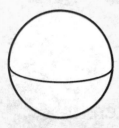 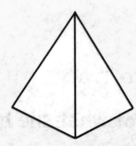 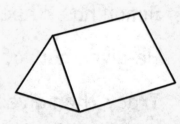

| sphere | square based pyramid | triangular prism |

1. Write the name of these 3 dimensional shapes :-

   (*Choose from* *cube, cuboid, cone, cylinder, sphere, pyramid, prism*).

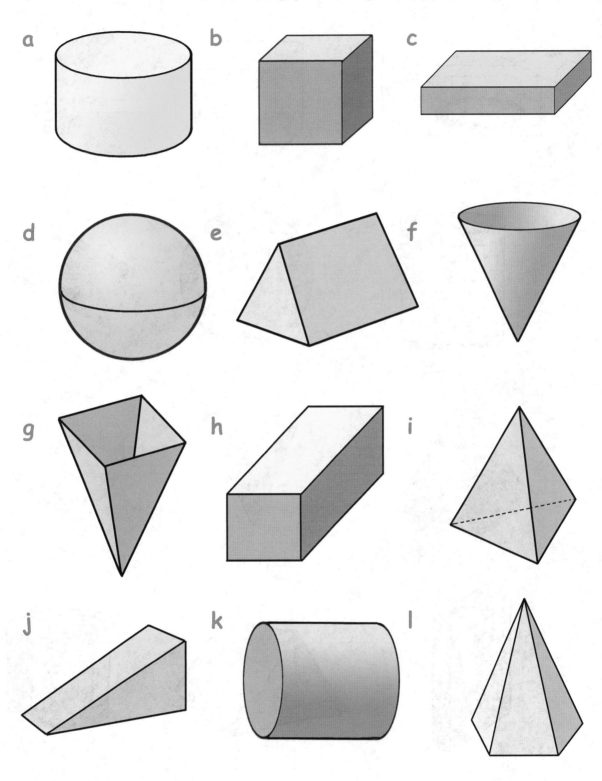

a   b   c

d   e   f

g   h   i

j   k   l

2. Here are some 3D items used in the real world.

(i)   Say what each object is.

(ii)   Write the name of each shape.

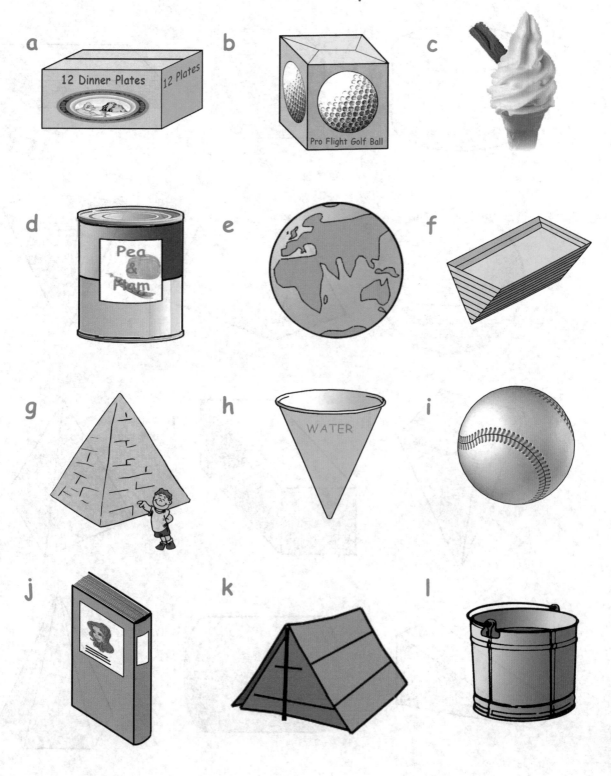

3. Make a list of the 3D shapes used in these pictures :-

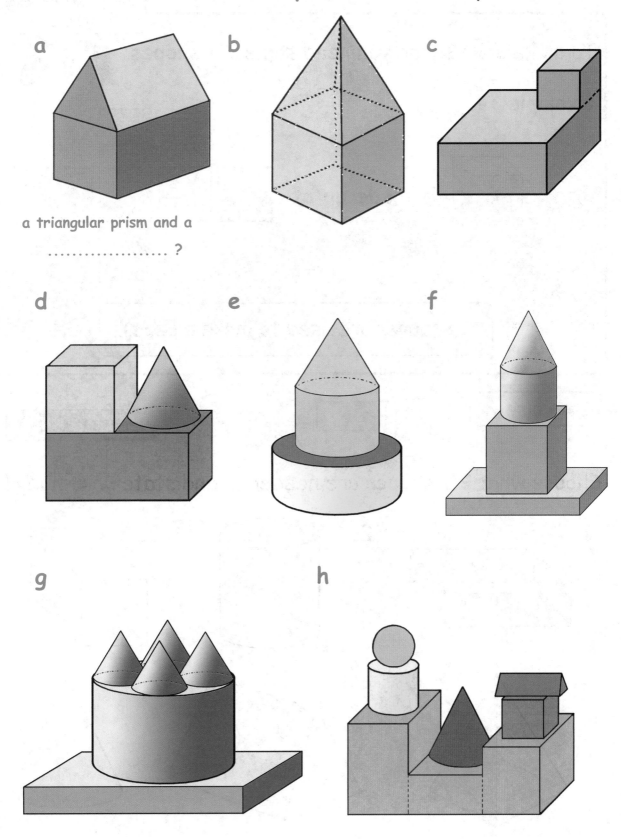

a

a triangular prism and a

.... ?

b

c

d

e

f

g

h

How to Make a 3D Shape

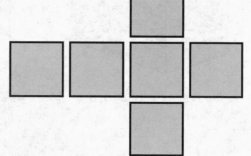

To make a 3D shape you need some 2D shapes.

Example :-

 is made up of

6 squares are used to make a cube.

Exercise 2 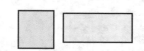  Worksheet 7·1

Choose what 2D shapes are needed ... and state how many !

1.
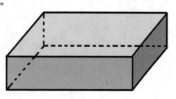

2.
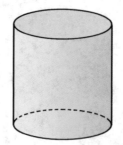

3.
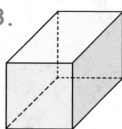

4.
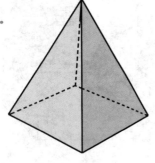

5.
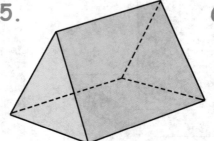

6.

1. What 3 dimensional shapes are these?

a    b 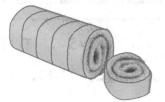   c

d    e 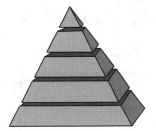   f

2. a Make a list of the 3D shapes in the diagram.

   b Write down how many of each you can see.

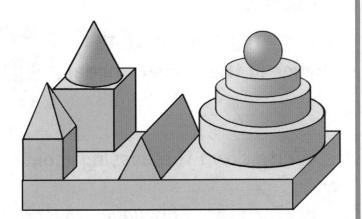

3. What 3D shape is made up of just 1 curved surface?

4. What hollow 3D shape is the red arrow pointing to?

It is NOT a cylinder.

5.

   a What 3D shape is this toilet roll?

   b How is a toilet roll made?

Months of the Year and Seasons

Learn the months and the seasons of the year.

You already know the days of the week. Can you remember them?

You will also need to know all the months of the year.

January	February	March
April	May	June
July	August	September
October	November	December

January
February
March
April
May
June
July
August
September
October
November
December

Exercise 1

1. Copy the months of the year in the correct order.

2. Write down the missing months :–

   a January, February, March, ...

   b June, July, ... , September

   c November, ... , January

   d April, ... , June, ... , ... , September

   e December, ... , February, ... , April

   f .... , October, ... , ... , ... , February.

3. a   What is the month just after March ?

   b   What is the month just before July ?

   c   What is the month just after September ?

   d   What is the month just before December ?

   e   What is the month just after April ?

   f   What is the month just before November ?

   g   What is the month just after February ?

   h   What is the month just before January ?

4.   What month is it :-

   a   2 months after June   b   2 months after September

   c   2 months before July   d   2 months before March

   e   3 months after December ?

5. a   What is the 3rd month of the year ?

   b   What is the 6th month of the year ?

   c   What is the last month of the year ?

Worksheet 8·1

You also need to know about the seasons of the year.

Spring $\longrightarrow$ Summer $\longrightarrow$ Autumn $\longrightarrow$ Winter

Discuss what kind of things happen
during each of the 4 seasons.

6. a Write the 4 seasons in order. Start with Winter.

   b In which season does the sun shine most ?

   c In which season does Christmas lie ?

7. *Extension.*
   a Use a calendar to find how many days there are in
      each month.

      For example, May has 31 days and June has 30 days.

   b Here is a small rhyme that tells you how many days
      there are in each month.

      > 30 days has September,
      > April, June and November.
      > All the rest have 31, except February,
      > which has 28 days clear,
      > and 29 days each leap year.

      Check that the rhyme works for each month.

Writing Dates

Be able to write and interpret dates.

The date, 3rd of January 2014

3rd Jan 2014

can be written using **6 digits**.

3rd January, 2014 $=$ 03 : 01 : 14 or 03/01/14

day   month   year

Exercise 2

1. Write each of these dates using **6 digits** as above :-

   a 23rd February 2014   b 19th April 2013

   c 22nd July 2014   d 18th August 2017

   e 7th June 2009   f 3rd March 2021

   g 10th December 2007   h 1st January 2016.

2. Write each of these dates as shown in question 1 :-

   a 14/01/13   b 01/03/14   c 11/11/11

   d 23/04/05   e 12:12:12   f 07:08:15

   g 09:03:20   h 31:06:16   i 30/02/10.

3. What is wrong with questions **2 h** and **2 i** above ?

Hours, Minutes and Seconds

Be aware of what units to use when measuring time.

If you wrote all the numbers from 1 to 30, it would take you about 1 minute.

1 minute is made up of 60 smaller bits called seconds.

You can measure seconds on a watch, stopwatch or by using a mobile phone.

1 hour = 60 minutes

1 minute = 60 seconds

Exercise 3

1. Would you measure these in hours, minutes or seconds :-

   a   the time taken to write the numbers 1 to 10

   b   the time taken to walk around the school building

   c   the time taken to drive from London to Glasgow ?

2. Match each action to one of these times :-

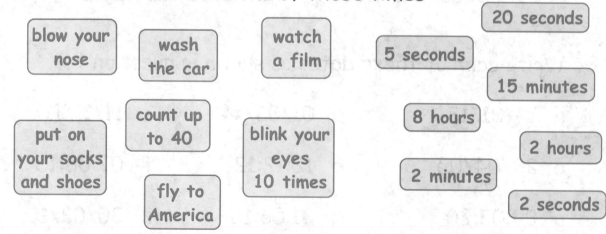

3. Ask your teacher if you can use a stopwatch or phone to time yourself doing some things.

1. Write down the **missing months** :-

   a April, ..., June, ...

   b December, January, ... , March

   c December, November, ... , September.

2. a What month comes just **after** February ?

   b What month comes just **before** January ?

   c What month is it **2 months after** August ?

3. Christmas comes in the winter time.

   a What **season** follows on **just after** winter ?

   b What is the **season just before** winter ?

4.  Write 31st May, 2015 using just **6 digits**.

5. Write out the date 28/10/16 in word form.

6. Would you measure these in **hours**, **minutes** or **seconds** :-

   a the time taken to fly from London to Rome

   b the time taken to walk up a flight of stairs

   c the time taken to swim 3 lengths of a swimming pool ?

Half of a Shape

Be able to recognise a half of a shape.

If you cut a shape into 2 equal bits, each bit is called a half.

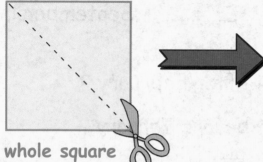

1 whole square

a half square

a half square

The square above has been cut in half.

Here, each half is a triangle.

Two halves put back together make one whole.

Exercise 1

1. Has this square been cut in half ?
   (Yes or No).

2. a Has this triangle
      been cut in half ?
      (Yes or No).

   b Has this circle been
      cut in half ? (Yes or No).

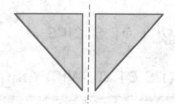

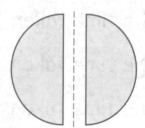

3. Has this rectangle been cut in **half** ?
(Yes or No).

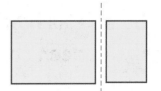

4. Which of these shapes have been cut **exactly** in half ?
(Yes or No).

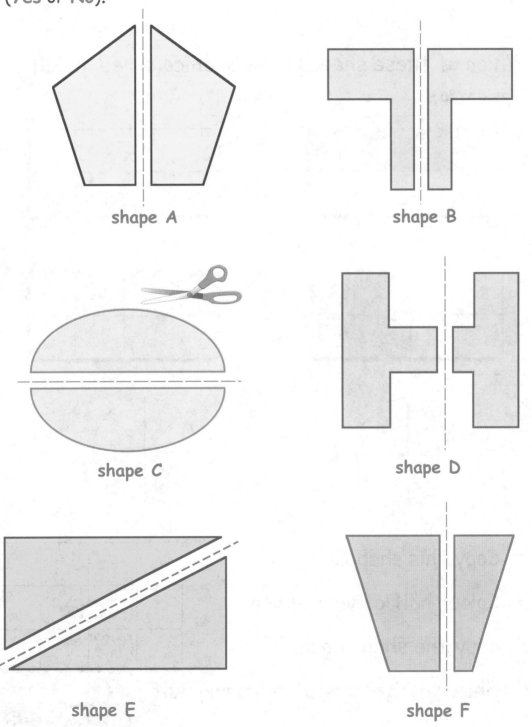

shape A

shape B

shape C

shape D

shape E

shape F

5. a Has **half** of this shape been coloured ?

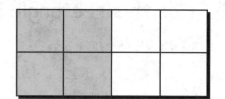

   b How many squares out of eight have been coloured ?

6. Which of these shapes have been coloured in **half** ? (Yes or No).

a 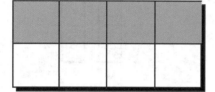 b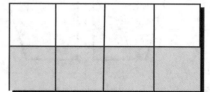

c 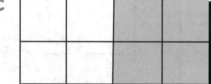 d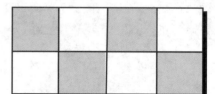

e 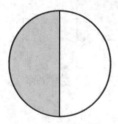 f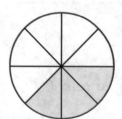

7. a Copy this shape.

   b Colour **half** of your shape.

   c Copy the shape again.

   d Show another way of colouring **half**.

Worksheet 9·1

Find a Half of Something

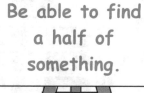

Be able to find a half of something.

1. Tim and Lorna had 10 sweets.

   They tried to share them equally.

Tim's sweets

Lorna's sweets

   a Did they each get exactly half of the sweets ?

   b How many sweets should each of them have ?

   c How many should Lorna give to Tim so that
      they do have half each ?

2. Andy shares 20 yellow counters with his friend James.

Andy   James

   a Did both boys get exactly half the counters ?

   b How many more did James get than Andy ?

3.  Bob and Bill share 14 toy cars.

They each get **half** of the cars.

How many cars does Bill get ?

4. Ari and Bree broke a bar of chocolate into 2 pieces.

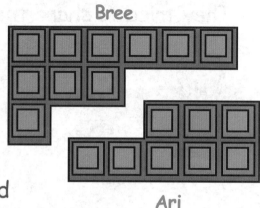

Bree

Ari

   a   Did both Ari and Bree get **exactly** half each ?

   b   How many **more** squares did Bree get than Ari ?

5. Julie and Janice share a bag of 12 balloons.

They each get exactly **half** of the balloons.

How many balloons did each girl get ?

6. Michael is walking from home to school.

 home   Michael    school

   a   Is Michael exactly **half** way to school ?

   b   Is he **more** than or is he **less** than **half** way to school ?

7. A box has ten toy soldiers.

Half of them them are taken out to play.

How many are left in the box ?

8. a   At a bus stop, there are eight people.

Half of them get on the first bus.

How many are now at the bus stop ?

b    Bronte has 16 tomatoes.

She uses half of them
for cooking.

How many does she use ?

c   A bag has twenty marbles.

Sadie is given half of them.

How many marbles are left in the bag ?

You might wish to use counters or cubes to help here.

9. a   Find a half of 6.   b   Find a half of 14.

c   Find a half of four.   d   Find a half of eighteen.

1. Trace or copy this shape.

   Draw a line to show how
   to find half of it.

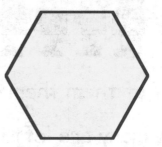

2. Which of these shapes have been cut exactly in half ?
   (Yes or No).

   a    b 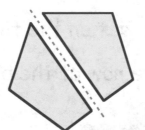   c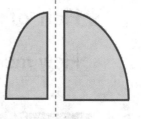

3. Copy or trace each shape and colour in a half :-

   a 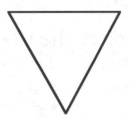   b 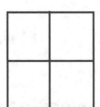   c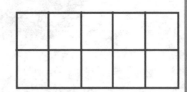

4. A bag has twenty sweets.

   Sean is given half of them.

   How many sweets are left in the bag ?

5. a   Find a half of 10.   b   Find a half of 16.

Chapter 10

Mass and Weight

Understand and use appropriate vocabulary in weight.

Words used in Mass or Weight

In **Chapter 3**, we used words like :-

longer - shorter - wider - narrower - taller - smaller.

When measuring **mass** or **weight**, we will use the words

lighter and **heavier**.

Examples :-

An elephant is heavier than a mouse.

A car is lighter than a bus.

Exercise 1

1. Which one is **lighter** :-

| a | a bush or a tree |  | b | a tiger or a dog |  |

c a desk or a chair   d a garden shed or a house

1. **e** a chair or a sofa   **f** a jet or a balloon

g a bed or a pillow   **h** a freezer or a microwave

i a fish or a chip   **j** a carrot or a turnip ?

2. Which one is **heavier** :-

a tennis ball or football

b robin or cat

c paper bag or shopping trolley

d beach ball or bowling ball

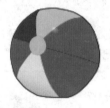

e train or bus   **f** desk light or street light

g bath or sink   **h** flower or bag of flour ?

3. Put these animals in order of weight.

   Start with the **lightest**.

| Frog | Goat | Bull | Dog |

4. Put these in order of weight. Start with the **heaviest**.

| Pencil | Desk | Chair | TJ Book |

5. Which of these is **heavier** :-

   a tomatoes or pineapple   b lemon or pepper ?

5. c   kiwi or grapes

d   watermelon or strawberry ?

6. Which of these is lighter :-

a   chilli or mushroom

b   red apple or green apple ?

7. I place a banana and a feather on the scales.

Which pan will go down - the pan with the banana or the pan holding the feather ?

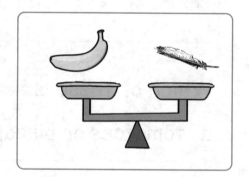

8.

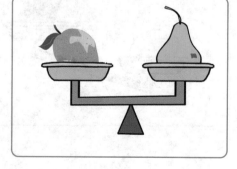

What can you say about the weights of the two fruits on these scales ?

Be able to
weigh objects
using scales.

*You need a set of scales and
some wooden cubes or marbles.*

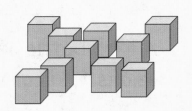

Your teacher will set out some objects for you to weigh.

You have to say how many wooden cubes or marbles it will take the scales to balance with each object.

Example :-

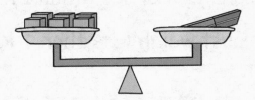

The small eraser weighs 6 cubes.

Exercise 2

Your teacher will set out some objects -
pens, pencils sharpeners, crayons,
calculators, dice, CD's etc.

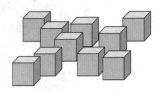

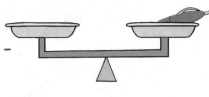

Weigh each of them and write
down your answers.

Measuring in Kilograms (kg)

Estimate whether an object is lighter or heavier than 1 kg.

When we weigh things, we often use **kilograms**.

> We can write **kilograms** as **kg**.

A **litre** bottle of limeade weighs 1 **kilogram**. (1 kg).

A bag of sugar weighs 1 kg.

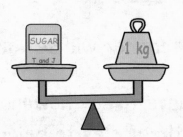

Does an apple weigh **more** or **less** than 1 kilogram ?

If it is **lighter** it must weigh less than 1 kg.

Exercise 3

1. Which is **lighter** ?

a

2 kg   3 kg

b

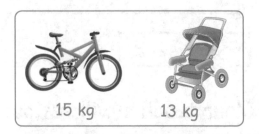

15 kg   13 kg

c

86 kg   45 kg

d

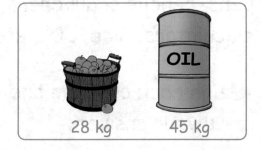

28 kg   45 kg

2. Put each list in order. Start with the **heaviest** :-

a   3 kg, 8 kg, 4 kg

b   9 kg, 11 kg, 14 kg, 10 kg

c   6 kg, 1 kg, 8 kg, 20 kg

d   23 kg, 31 kg, 27 kg, 30 kg

e   47 kg, 51 kg, 41 kg, 50 kg

f   70 kg, 81 kg, 69 kg, 89 kg, 75 kg.

3. a   Make a list of **ten** things that would be lighter than 1 kg.

b   Now make a list of **ten** things that would be **heavier** than 1 kg.

4. a   Find out how many kilograms you weigh.

b   Guess in kilograms, the weight of your TV.

c   Guess in kilograms, the weight of a cat.

Reading Scales

Be able to read the weight of an object on scales.

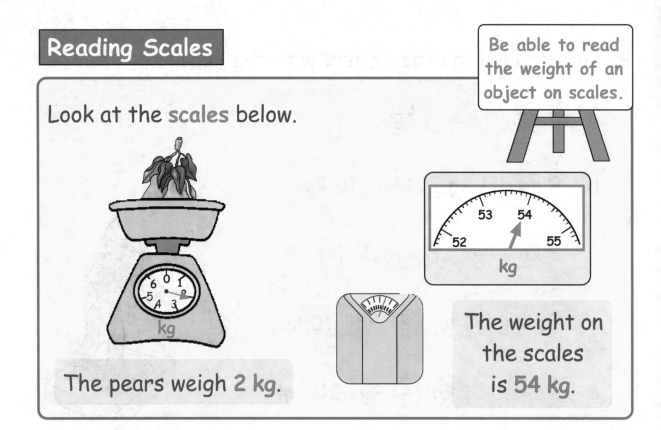

Look at the scales below.

The pears weigh 2 kg.

The weight on the scales is 54 kg.

Exercise 4

1. Write down the weight on each of these scales :-

a   b   c

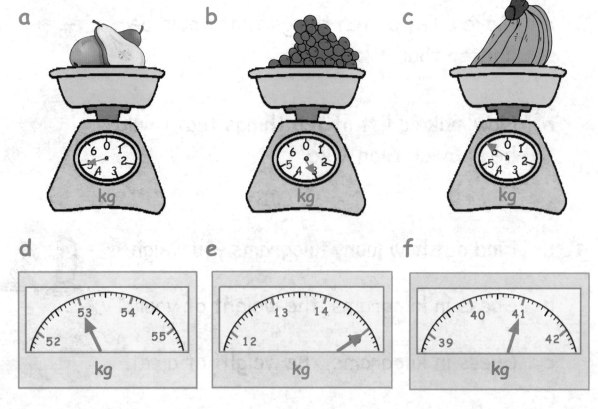

d   e   f

2. Write down the weight on each of these scales :-

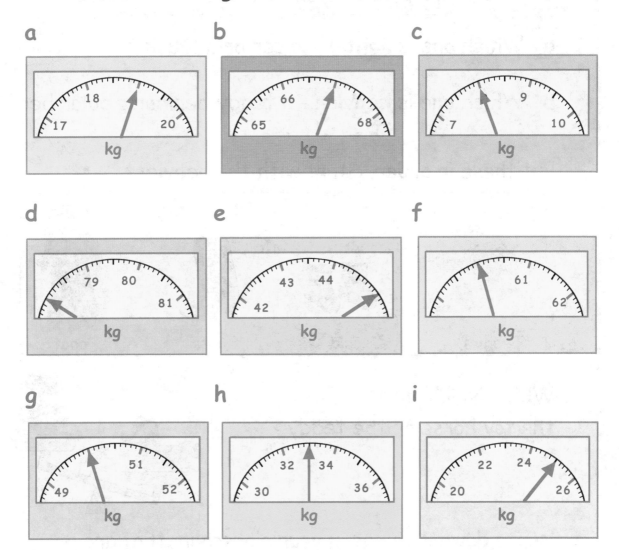

a

b

c

d

e

f

g

h

i

3. A bit trickier ! Write down the weight on each scale :-

a

b

c

1. a   Which one is lighter - a car or a truck ?

   b   Which one is heavier - a teddy bear or a polar bear ?

2. Put these in order. Start with the heaviest .

   T-shirt   socks   boots   coat

3. Which is lighter -
   the toy horse or the teddy ?

4. Write down 3 things in your classroom that are :-

   a lighter than 1 kilogram   b heavier than 1 kilogram.

5. Write down the weight on each of these scales :-

   a    b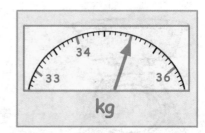

Chapter 11

A Quarter of a Shape

> Be able to identify a quarter of a shape.

If you cut a shape into 4 equal bits, each bit is called a quarter.

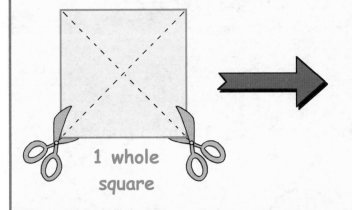

quarter

quarter

quarter

1 whole square

quarter

The square above has been cut into quarters.

Here, each quarter is a small triangle.

4 quarters put back together make a whole.

Two quarters put together make a half.

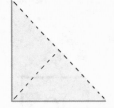

Exercise 1

1. Has this circle been cut into quarters ? (Yes or No).

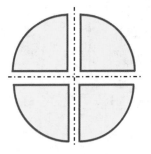

2. Has this rectangle been cut into quarters ?

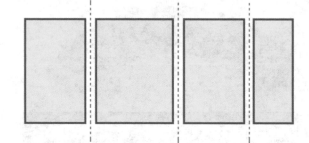

3. 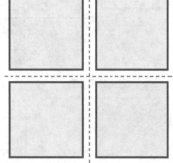 Has this square been cut into quarters ?

4. Which of these have been cut exactly into quarters ? (Yes or No).

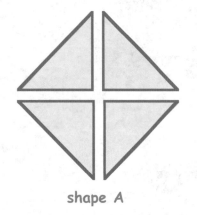

shape A

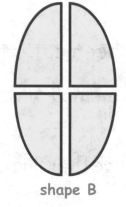

shape B

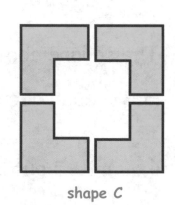

shape C

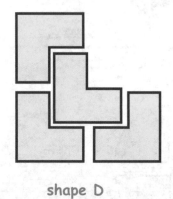

shape D

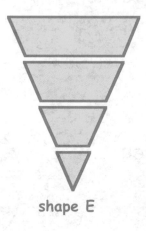

shape E

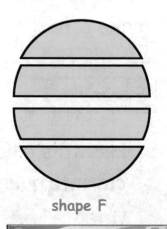

shape F

Worksheet 11·1

5. Jenny cut her birthday cake into 4 equal slices.

   Timmy ate one of the slices.

   What fraction did Timmy eat ?

6. Ben, Jane, Denzel and Lucy share some tennis balls.

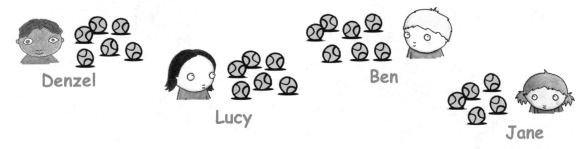

   Denzel

   Lucy

   Ben

   Jane

   a   Did each of them get a quarter of the balls ?

   b   Who got most ?

   c   Who got least ?

7. Mr Doak emptied a carton of limeade into 4 glasses.

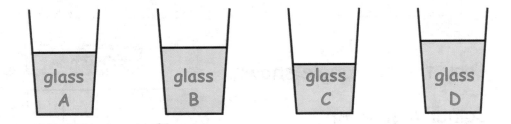

   glass A   glass B   glass C   glass D

   a   Did he pour exactly a quarter of the limeade
       into each glass ?

   b   Which glass held most ?

   c   Which glass held least ?

8. Which of these shapes have a **quarter** coloured ?
   (Yes or No).

   a

   b

   c

   d

   e

   f

   g

   h

9. a   Copy the rectangle shown.

    b   Colour a **quarter**
        of your shape.

    c   Copy it again.

    d   Show different ways to colour
        a **quarter** of your shape.

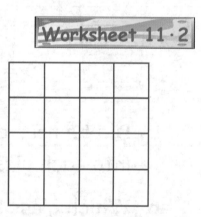

Mixed Exercise on a half and a quarter.

1. There are **12** pencils in a packet.

    a How many pencils would I have if I took **half** of them ?

    b How many pencils would I have if I took a **quarter** of them ?

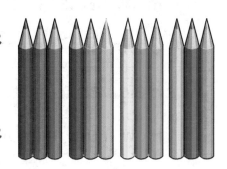

2.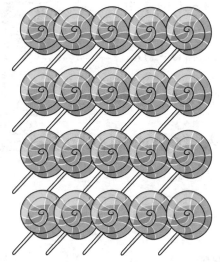

    There are **twenty** lollipops in a box.

    a How many lollipops would I have if I took **half** of them ?

    b How many lollipops would I have if I took a **quarter** of them ?

3. There are **16** golf balls in a bucket.

    a How many balls would I have if I took **half** of them ?

    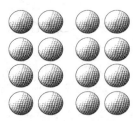

    b How many balls would I have if I took a **quarter** of them ?

4. a Max has 8 sweets.

   If he gives half to Sam, how many sweets will Sam have ?

   b Gavin has 8 marbles.

   He gives a quarter of them to Colin.

   How many marbles has he given to Colin ?

5. Caitlin had 16 flowers.

   a She gave half of the flowers to Una.

   How many flowers did she give to Una ?

   b She gave a quarter of her flowers to Mandy.

   How many flowers did she give to Mandy ?

6. Sara had twelve coins.

   She gave half of the coins to Dee.

   She also gave a quarter of the coins to Don.

   a How many coins did she give to Dee and to Don ?

   b How many did she have left ?

7. What is :-   a half of 6

   b half of 14   c half of 20

   d a quarter of 4   e a quarter of 20 ?

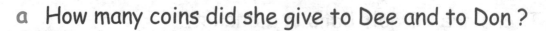

1. Trace or copy this shape.

   Draw lines to show how
   to find a quarter of it.

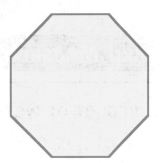

2. Which of these shapes have been
   cut exactly in quarters ? (Yes or No).

   a 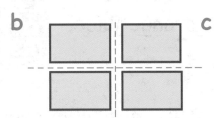   b 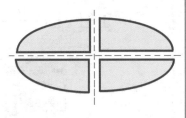   c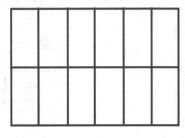

3. Copy or trace each shape and colour in a quarter :-

   a 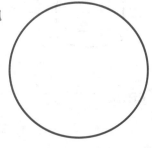   b 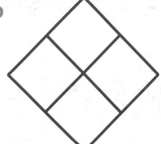   c

4. A bag has twenty sweets.

   Gabby is given a quarter of them.

   How many sweets has Gabby ?

5. a Find half of 12.   b Find a quarter of 12.

 **Chapter 12**

Liquid Measure

Be able to recognise if a container is full, half full etc.

The amount of water in a cup, jug, basin, barrel, etc. is called its **capacity** or **volume**.

Examples :-

This jug is **full** of orange juice.

 This jar is about **half full** of jam.

This bottle is **quarter full** of medicine.

 This jar of Pickles is **empty**.

Exercise 1

1. Are these jars **full**, **half full**, **quarter full** or **empty** ?

a    b    c 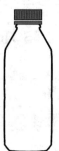   d

2. Which of these objects holds **more** :-

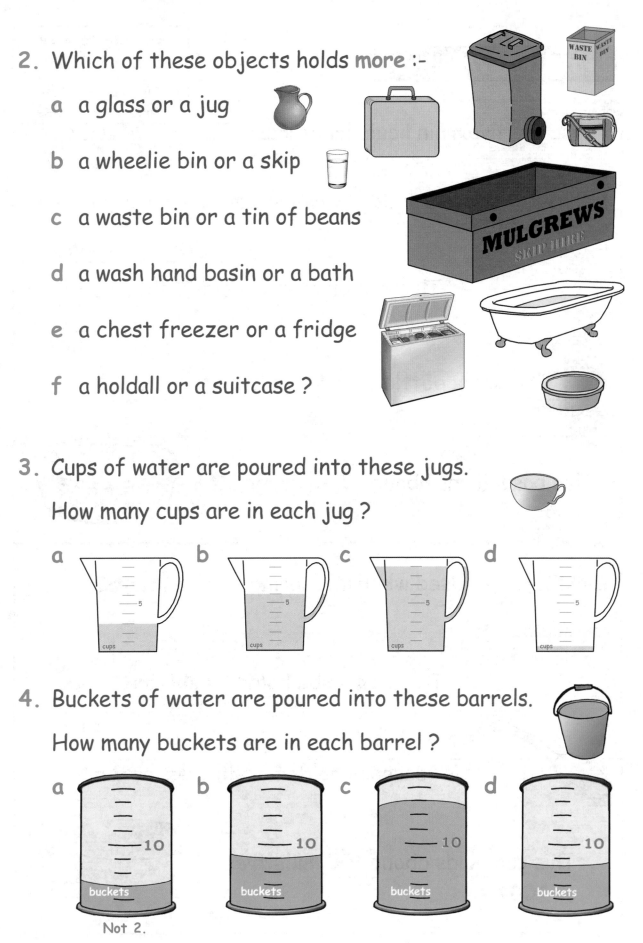

    a a glass or a jug

    b a wheelie bin or a skip

    c a waste bin or a tin of beans

    d a wash hand basin or a bath

    e a chest freezer or a fridge

    f a holdall or a suitcase ?

3. Cups of water are poured into these jugs.

   How many cups are in each jug ?

   a   b   c   d

4. Buckets of water are poured into these barrels.

   How many buckets are in each barrel ?

   a   b   c   d

   Not 2.

Litres and Millilitres

There are two main liquid measures.

Litres :- These are used when measuring large amounts.

Examples :-

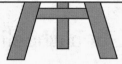

This carton of milk holds 1 litre.

This large bottle of cola holds 2 litres, or 2 *l*.

This basin holds about 10 litres, or 10 *l*.

Millilitres :- Used when measuring small amounts.

Examples :-

This 1 cm cube holds 1 millilitre.

This teaspoon holds 5 millilitres, or 5 *ml*.

This cup holds about 100 millilitres, or 100 *ml*.

1. What would you measure the water in this bucket in - litres or millilitres ?

2. What would you measure any liquid in this egg cup in - litres or millilitres ?

3. What would you use to measure these - ml or litres ?

a   b   c   d

e   f   g   h

4. Write these in order. Put the one that holds most first.

   bath - mug - tablespoon - saucer - sink - teapot.

5. Write in order. Put the one with the least water first.

   lake - sea - pond - puddle - raindrop - rain barrel.

6. How much liquid does each jar hold, (*in litres*) ?

a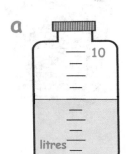

b

c

Not 5.

d

7. How much liquid, (*in millilitres (ml)*) ?

a

b

c

d

8. A medicine spoon holds **5 ml** of medicine.

   Denzel takes **3** spoonfuls each day.

   How much medicine does he take each day ?

9. A kettle holds **2 litres** of water when full.

   It takes **6** full kettles to fill a basin.

   How much water does the basin hold ?

1. Which holds more :-

   a   a swimming pool or a paddling pool

   b   a can of Cola or a carton of milk ?

2. How many buckets have been poured into the barrel ?

buckets

3. Would you use litres or millilitres for these ?

  a    b   c    d

4. Write these in order. Put the one that holds most first.

   water tank - bathroom sink - bath - shampoo bottle.

5. How much liquid does each jar hold ?

  a 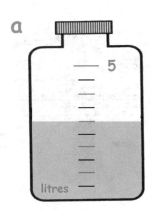   b 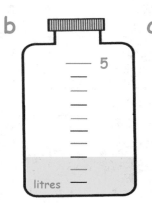   c    d

Position

Be able to understand left, right, up, down, on top of, beneath etc.

You can compare where 2 or more things are by using various words.

Discuss the following :-

↑ up
and
down ↓

left and right
← →

inside and outside
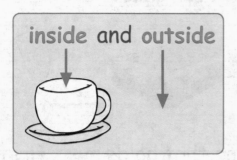

on top of →
and
beneath →

← top
← middle
← bottom

forwards and backwards

← behind
and
in front of

near and far

1. Which 2D shape is in front ?

a 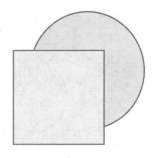   b 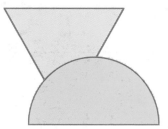   c

2. Which 3D shape is behind ?

a 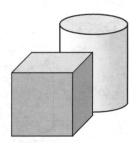   b 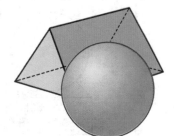   c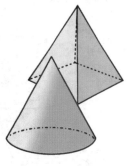

3. a Which boy is at the back ?

   b Which boy is at the front ?

   c Which boy is in the middle ?

Ben

Ravi

Nick

4.

a Which coin is at the back ?

b Which coin is at the front ?

c Which coin is in the middle ?

1. Which 2D shape is on top ?

a

b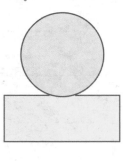

c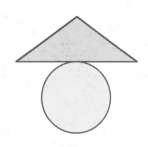

2. Which 3D shape is on the bottom ?

a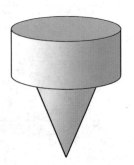

b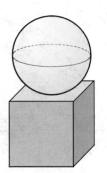

c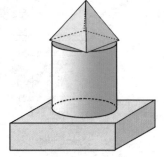

3. a   What is just above the plane ?

   b   What is just below the train ?

   c   What is on the middle shelf ?

4. Describe where these are :-

   a   the plane   b   the train

   c   the whistle   d   the spinning top.

Left and right

Left Hand   Right Hand

1. Which animal is on the **left** ?

a  b  c

2. Which fruit is on the **right** ?

a  b  c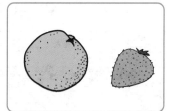

3.

a What lies just to the **left** of the doll ?

b What lies just to the **right** of the duck ?

c What lies on the very **left** ?

d What lies **3** places to the **right** of the toy soldier ?

You should know the words :-
     forward and **backwards**.

Example 1 :-

What colour will Jan end up on if she walks 7 squares **forward** then 2 squares **backwards** ?

Start here

She moves forward to **green** then back to red.

Example 2 :-

Give instructions for Pam to follow the path.

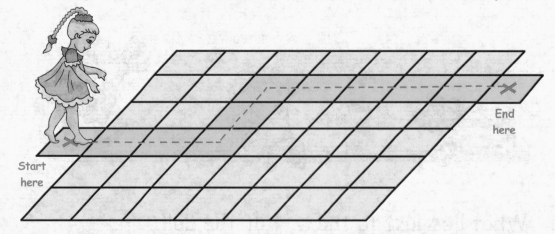

End here

Start here

Walk **3** slabs forward, then turn left.

Walk **2** slabs forward, then turn right.

Walk **5** slabs forward.

1. Willis is standing
   on the pink square.

forward

   a   Where will he be if he walks **4** squares forward ?

   b   Instead, Willis steps **2** squares backwards.

        Where does he then end up ?

   c   Willis starts on the light blue square, walks
        8 squares forward, then **4** squares backwards.

        On what square does he end up this time ?

2. Danny is standing at the bottom of this ladder.

   a   What colour of rung will he be on when
        he climbs **7** steps upwards ?

   b   Danny climbs up to the **black** rung.

        What must he then do to get
        to the white rung ?

   c   Danny starts from the ground.
        He climbs up **10** rungs.
        He then climbs down **7** rungs.

        On what rung colour does he end up ?

3. Give instructions
for Ben to follow
the path.

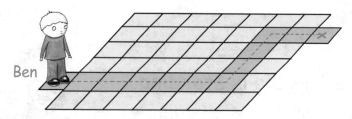

Start with -

Move ..... slabs f.........
Turn ....

4. Give instructions for Jane and Ella to follow these paths.

a

Jane

careful !

b

Ella

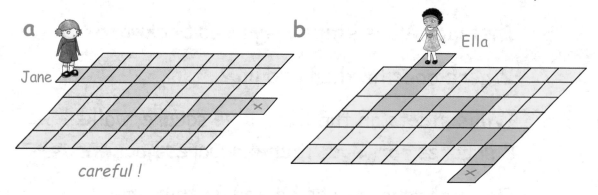

5. a   What will Nick find if he follows these instructions ?

Walk forward **5** slabs and turn left.
Walk forward **7** slabs and stop.

b   Give instructions for Nick to get to the :-

(i)   umbrella   (ii)   pram   (iii)   bike.

Quarter, Half and Three Quarter Turn

The hands of a clock move in a **clockwise** direction.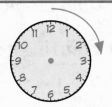

 **Anticlockwise** is the opposite direction.

quarter

Remember what a **quarter** looks like ?

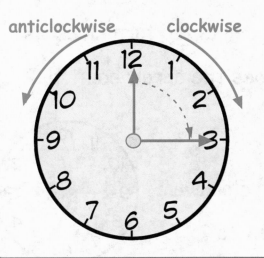

anticlockwise   clockwise

When the big hand moves **clockwise** from the **12** to the **3**, it has moved through a quarter turn clockwise.

Exercise 5

1. The blue arrow in the circle makes a **quarter** turn **clockwise**.

    Which shape is it pointing to ?

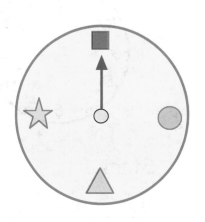

2. Instead, the blue arrow makes a **three quarter** turn **clockwise**.

    Which shape is it pointing to now ?

3. The arrow points at the green square and makes a **half** turn clockwise.

   Which shape is it pointing to now ?

4. The red arrow on the clock starts at 12.

   It makes a **quarter** turn clockwise.

   Where does the arrow then point to ?

5.

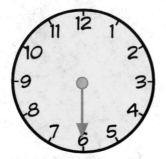

   Set the arrow to 6.

   It makes a **quarter** turn clockwise.

   Where does the arrow point to ?

6. The arrow points to 9.

   It makes a **three quarter** turn clockwise.

   Where will the arrow then point to ?

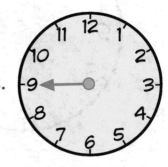

7.

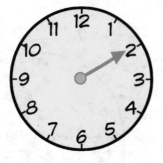

   Start at 2.

   Make a **full** turn clockwise.

   Where does the arrow point to ?

8. Start at 1.

   Make a **half** turn clockwise.

   Where does the arrow point to ?

9. Billy is standing at a crossroads.

   He is facing the church.

   Billy makes a quarter turn clockwise.

   What is Billy then looking at ?

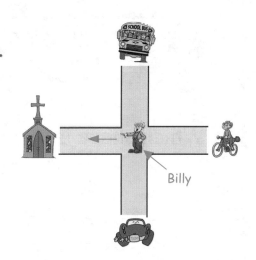

10. Billy faces the church. He makes a half turn clockwise.

    What is he then looking at ?

11. This time, Billy is facing the bus.

    He makes a three quarter turn clockwise.

    Where does he end up facing ?

12. A plane is flying towards a mountain.

    a   The plane makes a quarter turn clockwise.

        Where is the plane flying towards now ?

    b   The pilot then makes a half turn clockwise.

        Where is the plane then flying towards ?

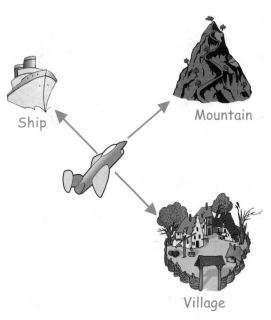

Ship

Mountain

Village

1. Which shape is **in front** ?

2. 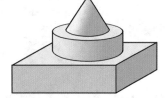   Which shape is **on the bottom** ?

3. a   Who is to the **left** of Jak ?

   b   Who is to the **right** of Paul ?

   c   Who is **just behind** Gary ?

4. Dave and Kim are playing Dragons and Dwarfs.

   a   Dave throws . Where does he land ?

   b   Kim throws [dice]. Where does she **finally** end up ?

5. Give instructions
   for Joe to follow
   the path.

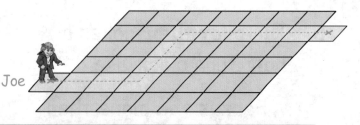

   Start with -   Move ..... slabs f......... . Turn ....

1. a Write all the numbers from 8 to 18 in order.

   b Write the numbers from 15 down to 10 in words.

2. Write these numbers in order. Put the largest first :-

   a 8, 11, 5, 14   b 17, 13, 14, 8, 19.

3. Write the number that is :-

   a 1 greater than 15   b 1 less than 10

   c 1 smaller than 19   d 1 more than 17.

4. Find the number between :-

   a 18 and 20   b 13 and 11.

5. Write down all the numbers between 13 and 20.

6. Name these 2 dimensional shapes :-

   a    b    c 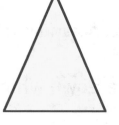   d

7. a How many **edges** has a square ?

   b How many **sides** has a triangle ?

   c How many **corners** has a circle ?

8. Copy and fill in all the missing numbers :-

   a 7   8   9   ☐   11   ☐   ☐   14   15

   b 4   6   ☐   10   12   ☐   16   18   ☐

   c 63 62 ☐ 60 ☐ 58 57 ☐ 55

   d 35 ☐ 45 50 ☐ 60 ☐ 70 ☐

   e 39 37 ☐ 33 ☐ 29 ☐ ☐ 23.

9. a What does the **2** stand for in the number 26 ?

   b What does the **9** stand for in the number 89 ?

10. Look at these numbers - 37, 24, 91, 30, 75, 59, 62.

   a Write down which of the numbers are **even**.

   b Write down which of them are **odd** numbers.

11. Put these numbers in order, smallest number first :-

a 28, 39, 32, 41   b 46, 30, 51, 50

c 74, 25, 45, 42   d 88, 33, 55, 27.

12. a Which day of the week comes just after Monday ?

b Which day comes just before Saturday ?

c If today is Sunday, what will tomorrow be ?

13. What is the missing month in each of these :-

a March, ..., May   b July, ..., September ?

14. In which month is New Year's day ?

15. Say in which season each of these would take place :-

a    b

Autumn
Summer
Winter
Spring

16. Which season comes just after Winter ?

17. The buses are lined up in order.

What are the missing bus numbers ?

18. What times are shown on these clocks ?

a    b 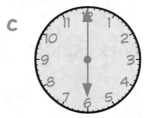   c    d

19. Write down the value of each of these :-

a    b    c

d    e    f

20. Write down the answers to the following :-

a   4 + 3   b   8 + 5   c   6 + 9

d   13 + 4   e   12 + 7   f   2 + 18

g   3 + 4 + 5   h   5 + 5 + 6   i   9 + 8 + 3.

21. Write down the answers to the following :-

a   5 – 3   b   9 – 2   c   10 – 5

d   12 – 4   e   13 – 10   f   15 – 1

g   16 – 2 – 3   h   9 – 4 – 5   i   20 – 7 – 3.

22. How much does each girl have ?

Jo

Liane

Avril

23. Which coins could I use to pay for these exactly :-

a

9p

b

14p

c

18p

24. When a dart lands on a blue section your score is doubled.

What did Eric score with his dart ?

Eric

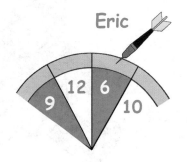

12 6

9   10

25.  Share these pins equally between Beth and Joshua so they each get the same number.

26. Draw or trace this rectangle.

Colour or shade in half of the rectangle.

27. 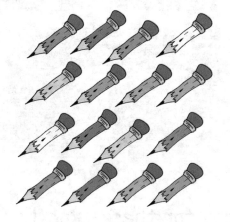 I have 16 pencils.

I gave away half of them to my friend.

How many do I have left ?

28. Draw or trace this shape.

Colour or shade in a quarter of the shape.

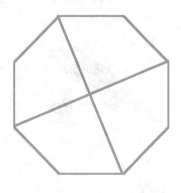

29.  This teddy has 7 buttons.

How many buttons will there be on two identical teddies ?

30. This cake has been cut into equal pieces.

   a   How many pieces ?

   b   Jake ate a quarter of it.

   How many pieces did Jake eat ?

31. Which tree is taller - the apple tree or the cherry tree ?

apple   cherry

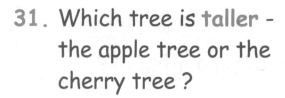

32.

Which is flying lower - the plane or the balloon ?

33. a   Use a ruler to measure the length and width, of this rectangle, in centimetres, *to the nearest cm.*

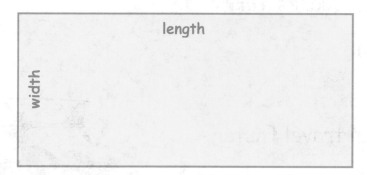

length

width

   b   Which is longer - the length or the width ?

34. The arrow in this spinner points to the letter a.

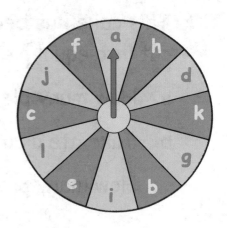

   a   The arrow is spun a **half-turn**.

        What letter does it end up pointing to ?

   b   This time, the arrow starts at the letter a and makes a **three quarters** turn to the **left**.

        What letter does it now end up pointing to ?

35. This chess piece is moved around the board.

Copy and complete :-

Move ...... squares **forward**.

Turn r.........

Move ...... squares **forward**.

Turn ....

Move ...... squares **forward**.

and finish.

36. Which can travel **faster** -

a helicopter or a jet plane ?

37.    Which is **heavier** - the milk or the raspberry juice ?

38. a   Which jar is **quarter** full - yellow, red or green ?

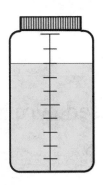 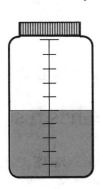 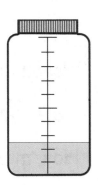

b   What can you say about the jar with the **red** liquid ?

39. Draw the shape that is missing in this pattern :-

....

40. Draw the next shape in this pattern :-

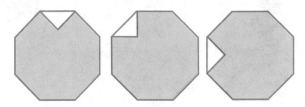 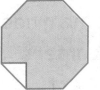

....

41. What is the next number :-   25   30   35   40   45   .... ?

42. Write down what 3D shapes
you can see here and say
how many of each there are.

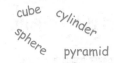

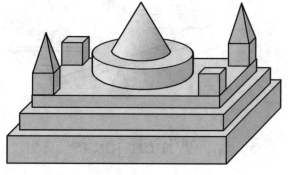

43. a   How many **faces** has a cuboid ?

    b   How many **edges** has a square based pyramid ?

    c   How many **corners** has a cylinder ?

44. 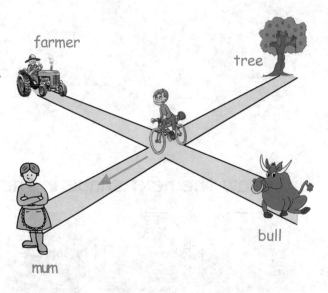   Lucy has 17p and Jane has 8p.

    How much **more** has Lucy than Jane ?

45. Billy is cycling home.

    He is at the crossroads.

    a   What would Billy
    be looking at if he
    made a **half** turn ?

    b   If instead, he made
    a **three quarters**
    turn to his left,
    who would he see ?

Answers to Year 1 Book 1B

Chapter 1 - Addition/Subtraction - Page 1

Ch 1 - Exercise 1 - Page 1

1. 8
2. a 13   b 15   c 16
   d 17   e 18   f 19
   g 10   h 19   i 20
3. a 8   b 5   c 9
   d 8   e 2   f 4
4. 19
5. 18.
6. 19.
7. 20
8. 19

Ch 1 - Exercise 2 - Page 3

1. a 5   b 3   c 3
2. a 11   b 14   c 11
   d 10   e 4   f 6
   g 5   h 9   i 7
3. a 12   b 11   c 10
   d 7   e 12   f 12
   g 7   h 12   i 0
4. 11
5. 12
6. 9
7. a 7   b 8
8. a 4   b 9   c 13
   d 9   e 16   f 7
9. 18

Ch 1 - Exercise 3 - Page 5

1. a 10   b 2   c 9   d 2
2. a 12   b 16   c 13
   d 20   e 8   f 19
   g 8   h 20   i 9
3. a 18   b 14   c 16   d 5
   e 18   f 9   g 5   h 7
4. 6
5. 7
6. 7
7. 5

8. 8
9. a 9   b 7   c 10
   d 8   e 20   f 8
10. 11

Chapter 2 - Grouping - Page 8

Ch 2 - Exercise 1 - Page 9

1. a 3   b 6   c 2 lots of 3 are 6
2. a 4   b 8   c 2 lots of 4 are 8
3. a 6   b 12   c 2 lots of 6 are 12
4. a 7p   b 14p   c 2 lots of 7 are 14
5. a 8   b 16   c 2 lots of 8 are 16
6. a 10   b 20   c 2 lots of 10 are 20
7. a 2   b 4
8. a 6   b 8   c 10   d 12
   e 14   f 16   g 18   h 20
   i 22   j 24
9. a 2 4 6 8 10 12 14 16 18 20
   b Go up in 2's: Even
10. a 8   b 14
11. a 16   b 20   c 18   d 10
12. 12
13. a 22   b 9

Ch 2 - Exercise 2 - Page 13

1. a 4   b 6   c 8
   d 10   e 12   f 14
   g 16   h 18   i 20
2. a 1   b 8   c 10
   d 14   e 12

Chapter 3 - Length & Height - Page 15

Ch 3 - Exercise 1 - Page 17

1. a B   b A
2. a C   b D
3. a E   b E
4. a G   b H
5. a J   b J   c twice   d half
6. a L   b K

7. Rita
8. Daisy

Ch 3 - Exercise 2 - *Page 19*

1. Various
2. Various
3. Various - yardstick
4. one person's hand is not same size
    as everyone else !

Chapter 4 - Patterns - *Page 22*

Ch 4 - Exercise 1 - *Page 23*

1. a 0 2 4 6 8 10 12
    b 0 2 4 6 8 10 12 14 16 18 20
       22 24 26 28 30
2. a 1 3 5 7 9 11
    b 1 3 5 7 9 11 13 15 17 19 21
       23 25 27 29 31 33 35 37 39
       41 43 45 47 49
3. a 24 26 28   b 24 22 20
    c 57 59 61   d 83 81 79
    e 80 82 84   f 69 67 65
4. a 14 20   b 19 25
    c 35 43   d 80 72
    e 91 85   f 66 72 74
5. 37 41 43   6. 70 74 76
7. 60   8. 88
9. 29 33

Ch 4 - Exercise 2 - *Page 26*

1. a 0 5 10 15 20
    b 0 5 10 15 20 25 30 35 40 45 50
2. a 60 65 70 75
    b 60 65 70 75 80 85 90 95 100
3. a 25 30 35   b 50 55 60
    c 15 10 5   d 60 55 50
    e 10 5 0   f 85 80 75
4. a 10 20   b 40 50
    c 25 10   d 40 35
    e 70 85   f 95 75
5. a 0 10 20 30
    b 0 10 20 30 40 50 60 70 80 90 100
6. a 60 70   b 90 100
    c 10 0   d 70 60

7. a 10 40   b 50 80
    c 30 20   d 90 60
8. a 13 23 33 43 53 63 73 83
    b 97 87 77 67 57 47 37
9. a 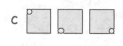   b
    c   d
10. a   b
    c   d

Ch 4 - Exercise 3 - *Page 30*

1. a 5 7 9 11 13 15 17 19 21 23 25
1. b 8 10 12 14 16 18 20 22 24 26 28 30
2. a even   b odd
3. 7
4. a even   b even   c odd   d odd
    e even   f even   g odd   h odd
5. a 8 24 52 66   b 35 49 87
6. even - always even

Chapter 5 - Length & Height - *Page 32*

Ch 5 - Exercise 1 - *Page 32*

1. a 7 cm   b 12 cm   c 3 cm
    d 9 cm   e 15 cm   f 14 cm
2. a 13 cm   b 8 cm   c 11 cm
    d 4 cm   e 12 cm   f 6 cm
3. a 5 cm   b 4 cm   c 2 cm
    d 8 cm   e 14 cm
4. a 19 cm   b 27 cm   c/d Various guesses
5. Measurements
6. Check lengths of lines in drawings
7. a length 3 cm   width 3 cm
    b length 7 cm   width 4 cm
    c length 14 cm   width 2 cm
8. Check drawings
9. Check drawings

Ch 5 - Exercise 2 - *Page 36*

1. Various guesses
2. Measurements.

Ch 6 - Exercise 1 - *Page 39*

1. a 3
2. a 8 cubes   b share out   c 4 each
3. a 10 cubes   b share out   c 5 each
4. b 6 each
5. b 7 each
6 b 8 each
7. a 3 each b 4 each
8. a 5   b 9   c 6
9. a 3   b 1
10. a 4   b 1
11. a 10   b 6
    c 8   d 20
12. a 2   b 3   c 6
    d 1   e 5   f 0
13. 10p
14. 8

Chapter 7 - 3 Dimensions - *Page 44*

Ch 7 - Exercise 1 - *Page 45*

1. a cylinder   b cube
   c cuboid   d sphere
   e triangular prism f cone
   g square based pyramid
   h cuboid
   i triangle based pyramid
   j triangular prism k cylinder
   l prism
2. a box of plates - cuboid
   b box with 1 golf ball - cube
   c 99 ice cream cone - cone
   d tin of soup - cylinder
   e world globe - sphere
   f water trough - triangular prism
   g pyramid - pyramid
   h water cup - cone
   i baseball - sphere
   j book - cuboid
   k tent - triangular prism
   l bucket - cylinder

3. a triangular prism and cuboid
   b pyramid and cube
   c cuboid and cube
   d cuboid, cube and cone
   e 2 cylinders and a cone
   f cylinder, cone, cuboid and cube
   g 4 cones, a cylinder and a cuboid
   h 1 sphere, 1 cylinder, 3 cuboids, 1 cone
      1 cube and 1 triangular prism

Ch 7 - Exercise 2 - *Page 48*

1. 6 rectangles
2. 1 rectangle & 2 circles
3. 2 squares & 4 rectangles
4. 1 square & 4 triangles
5. 2 triangles & 3 rectangles
6. 1 circle & a part of a larger circle (sector)

Chapter 8 - Time 2 - *Page 50*

Ch 8 - Exercise 1 - *Page 50*

1. January, February, March, April, May,
    June, July, August, September, October,
    November, December
2. a April   b August c December
    d May, July, August e January, March
    f September November December January
3. a April   b June
    c October   d November
    e May   f October
    g January   h December
4. a August   b November
    c May   d January
    e March
5. a March b June   c December
6. a Winter - Spring - Summer - Autumn
    b Summer   c Winter
7. a Jan (31)   Feb (28*) Mar (31)
       Apr (30)   May (31)   Jun (30)
       Jul (31)   Aug (31)   Sep (30)
       Oct (31)   Nov (30)   Dec (31)   *or 29
    b Learn rhyme and check it works

Ch 8 - Exercise 2 - *Page 53*

1. a 23:02:14   b 19:04:13
   c 22:07:14   d 18:08:17
   e 07:06:09   f 03:03:21
   g 10:12:07   h 01:01:16
2. a 14th Jan 2013   b 1st Mar 2014
   c 11th Nov 2011   d 23rd Apr 2005
   e 12th Dec 2012   f 7th Aug 2015
   g 9th Mar 2020   h 31st Jun 2016
   i 30th Feb 2010
3. 2h there are only 30 days in June 2016
   2i there are only 28 days in Feb 2010

Ch 8 - Exercise 3 - *Page 54*

1. a secs   b mins   c hours
2. blow nose - 2 secs   wash car - 15 mins
   watch film - 2 hrs   socks/shoes - 2 mins
   count to 40 - 20 secs   fly to America - 8 hrs
   blink eyes 10 times - 5 secs
3. Practical

Chapter 9 - Fractions 1 - *Page 56*

Ch 9 - Exercise 1 - *Page 56*

1. Yes
2. a Yes   b Yes
3. No
4. A Yes   B Yes   C Yes
   D No   E Yes   F No
5. a Yes   b 4
6. a Yes   b Yes   c Yes
   d Yes   e Yes   f No
7. see diagrams

Ch 9 - Exercise 2 - *Page 59*

1. a No   b 5   c 1
2. a No   b 2
3. 7
4. a No   b 2
5. 6
6. a No   b more
7. 5
8. a 4   b 8   c 10
9. a 3   b 7   c 2   d 9

Chapter 10 - Mass and Weight - *Page 63*

Ch 10 - Exercise 1 - *Page 63*

1. a bush   b dog   c chair
   d shed   e chair   f balloon
   g pillow   h microwave
   i chip   j carrot
2. a football   b cat
   c shopping trolley   d bowling ball
   e train   f street light
   g bath   h bag of flour
3. Frog, dog, goat, bull
4. Desk, chair, book, pencil
5. a pineapple   b lemon
5. c grapes   d watermelon
6. a chilli   b green apple
7. banana (left side)
8. they are the same weight

Ch 10 - Exercise 2 - Practical - *Page 67*

Ch 10 - Exercise 3 - *Page 68*

1. a teapot - 2 kg   b push chair - 13 kg
   c woman - 45 kg   d apples - 28 kg
2. a 8 kg, 4 kg, 3 kg
   b 14 kg, 11 kg, 10 kg, 9 kg
   c 20 kg, 8 kg, 6 kg, 1 kg
   d 31 kg, 30 kg, 27 kg, 23 kg
   e 51 kg, 50 kg, 47 kg, 41 kg
   f 89 kg, 81 kg, 75 kg, 70 kg, 69 kg
3. a Check list   b Check list
4. Various answers

Ch 10 - Exercise 4 - *Page 70*

1. a 5 kg   b 3 kg   c 6 kg
   d 53 kg   e 15 kg   f 41 kg
2. a 19 kg   b 67 kg   c 8 kg
   d 78 kg   e 45 kg   f 60 kg
   g 50 kg   h 33 kg   i 25 kg
3. a 2 kg   b 8 kg
   c 23 and a half kg

Chapter 11 - Fractions 2 - *Page 73*

Ch 11 - Exercise 1 - *Page 73*

1. Yes
2. No
3. Yes
4. A Yes   B Yes   C Yes
   D Yes   E No   F No
5. one quarter
6. a No   b Ben   c Jane
7. a No   b Glass B
   c Glass C
8. a Yes   b Yes   c Yes   d Yes
   e Yes   f No   g Yes   h No
9. Check diagrams

Ch 11 - Exercise 2 - *Page 77*

1. a 6   b 3
2. a 10   b 5
3. a 8   b 4
4. a 4   b 2
5. a 8   b 4
6. a 6 and 3   b 3
7. a 3   b 7   c 10
   d 1   e 5

Chapter 12 - Volume/Capacity - *Page 80*

Ch 12 - Exercise 1 - *Page 80*

1. a half full   b full
   c empty   d quarter full
2. a jug   b skip   c waste bin
   d bath   e freezer f suitcase
3. a 3   b 6   c 9   d half
4. a 4   b 8   c 16   d 7

Ch 12 - Exercise 2 - *Page 83*

1. litres
2. millilitres
3. a litres   b millilitres
   c litres   d millilitres
   e millilitres   f litres
   g millilitres   h litres

4. Bath, sink, teapot, mug,
   saucer, tablespoon
5. Raindrop, puddle, rain barrel,
   pond, lake, sea
6. a 6 litres   b 5 litres
   c 2 and a half litre d half a litre
7. a 15 ml   b 33 ml   c 48 ml   d 6 ml
8. 15 ml
9. 12 litres

Chapter 13 - Position & Direction - *Page 86*

Ch 13 - Exercise 1 - *Page 87*

1. a square   b semi circle
   c star
2. a cylinder   b triangular prism
   c square based pyramid
3. a Ben   b Nick   c Ravi
4. a 50p   b 5p   c 20p

Ch 13 - Exercise 2 - *Page 88*

1. a square b circle c triangle
2. a cone   b cube   c cuboid
3. a whistle   b jack in the box
   c spinning top
4. a 2nd top, just below whistle, etc
   b 2nd bottom, just below top, etc
   c very top, just above plane, etc
   d middle, just above train, etc

Ch 13 - Exercise 3 - *Page 89*

1. a pig   b sheep   c cat
2. a apple   b grapes c strawberry
3. a soldier b horse   c teddy   d horse

Ch 13 - Exercise 4 - *Page 91*

1. a grey   b green   c pink
2. a green   b down 5 c yellow
3. Move 6 forward, turn left,
   move 3 forward, turn right,
   move 2 forward.
4. a Move 3 forward, turn right,
       move 3 forward, turn left,
       move 3 forward, turn left,
       move 1 forward, turn right, 2 forward.

4. b Move 3 forward, turn left,
       move 3 forward, turn right,
       move 2 forward, turn left,
       move 2 forward, turn right,
       move 2 forward.
5. a ball
    b (i) Walk forwards 7 slabs,
            turn right, forward 5,
            turn left forward 1.
       (ii) Forward 10, turn left,
             forward 3, turn right,
             forward 3.
       (iii) Forward 12, turn right,
              forward 4, turn left,
              forward 3.

Ch 13 - Exercise 5 - Page 93

1. pink circle   2. Yellow star
3. blue triangle   4. 3
5. 9   6. 6
7. 2   8. 7
9. bus   10. bicycle
11. church
12. a village b ship

Chapter 14 - Revision Year 1 - Page 97

1. a 8, 9, 10, 11, 12, 13, 14, 15, 16, 17, 18
    b Fifteen, fourteen, thirteen,
       twelve, eleven, ten
2. a 14, 11, 8, 5   b 19, 17, 14, 13, 8
3. a 16   b 9   c 18   d 18
4. a 19   b 12
5. 13, 14, 15, 16, 17, 18, 19, 20
6. a square   b rectangle
    c triangle   d circle
7. a 4   b 3   c 0
8. a 10, 12, 13   b 8, 14, 20
    c 61, 59, 56   d 40, 55, 65, 75
    e 35, 31, 27, 25
9. a tens   b units (ones)
10. a 24, 30, 62   b 37, 91, 75, 59
11. a 28, 32, 39, 41   b 30, 46, 50, 51
    c 25, 42, 45, 74   d 27, 33, 55, 88
12. a Tuesday   b Friday
    c Monday

13. a April   b August
14. January
15. a Summer   b Spring
16. Spring
17. 40, 46
18. a 8 o'clock   b half past two
    c 6 o'clock   d half past ten
19. a 3p   b 7p   c 11p
    d 30p   e 52p   f 65p
20. a 7   b 13   c 15
    d 17   e 19   f 20
    g 12   h 16   i 20
21. a 2   b 7   c 5
    d 8   e 3   f 14
    g 11   h 0   i 10
22. Jo has 9p. Liane 16p. Avril £18
23. a 5p, 2p, 2p   b 10p, 2p, 2p
    c 10p, 5p, 2p, 1p
24. 12
25. 7 each
26. Check diagram
27. 8
28. Check diagram
29. 14
30. a 12   b 3
31. apple
32. balloon
33. a length 9 cm, breadth 4 cm
    b length
34. a i   b k
35. Move 4 squares forward. Turn right.
    Move 5 squares forward. Turn left.
    Move 2 squares forward.
36. jet-plane
37. milk
38. a green   b half full
39.   40.

41. 50
42. Cone 1,   cylinder 1,   pyramid 2,
    cubes 4   cuboids 3.
43. a 6   b 8   c 0
44. 9p
45. a tree   b farmer.